Colourful Dar...

Chips Barber

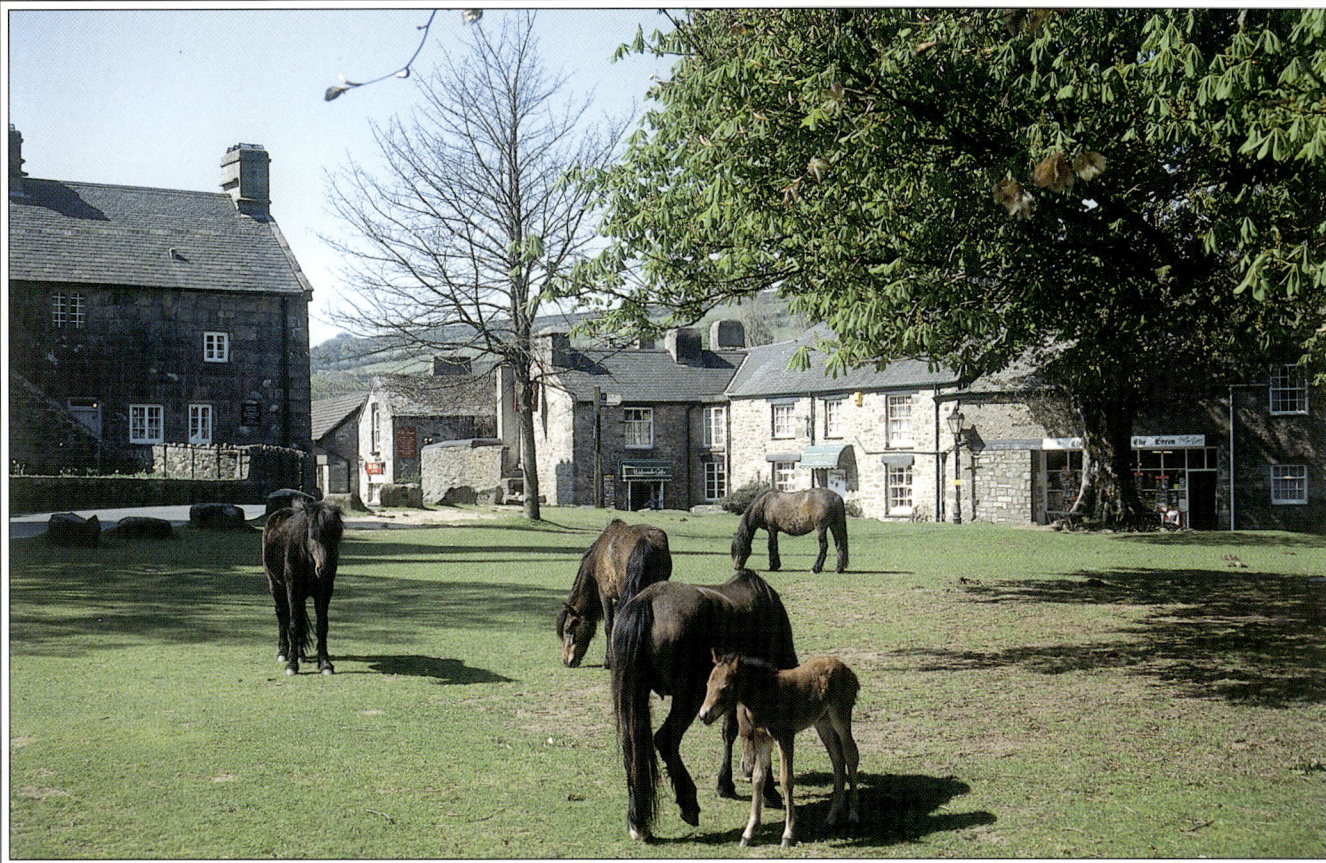

Old Uncle Tom Cobley ...

Above is the village green of Widecombe-in-the-Moor, a place many folk have heard of because of its legendary folk song starring Bill Brewer, Jan Stewer, Peter Gurney, Peter Davey, Dan'l Whiddon, Harry Hawk, Old Uncle Tom Cobley and all! Opposite right is a well-read 'Old Grey Mare' ridden by 'Old Uncle Tom Cobley'. The picture was taken at the annual Widecombe Fair, held on the second Tuesday in September, an event which always draws large crowds. Opposite left is a picture taken at Bovey Tracey, nicknamed 'The Gateway to Dartmoor' and located on the River Bovey.

Widecombe-in-the-Moor

This is a view of the village as seen from the top of the long, steep Widecombe Hill. The church tower of St Pancras, often referred to as 'the Cathedral of the Moor', makes a bold landmark. Shown opposite is one of Dartmoor's more unusual features, the queer rock idol of Bowerman's Nose, which is on the side of Hayne Down, not far from Hound Tor. The far right photo is of the unique Haytor Granite Tramway, where the lines were made from granite and installed for the transport of the same rock, there once being many granite quarries in the vicinity of Haytor Rock, seen in the distance.

Haytor Rock

This enormous outcrop lies close to the Bovey Tracey to Widecombe road and has long been a favourite of both locals and visitors alike. From its summit, on a good day, there are far-ranging views: it's possible to see part of the South Hams, Berry Head at Brixham, most of Torbay, Little Haldon, the Haldon Hills and parts of both North and East Devon.

A Touching Memorial

Here is a cross set up on a small isolated rock at the foot of Corndon Tor, to the memory of 18-year-old Evelyn Anthony Cave Penny, who was killed on 8 June 1918 by a sniper's bullet during the Great War. He grew up at Sherwell, an ancient farm about a mile away in the nearby East Dart valley. The cross stands on a rock known as 'The Belstone Bible'. The tor in the distance is Yar Tor, which overlooks Dartmeet.

Lustleigh

The pictures on these two pages are both of Lustleigh, one of the prettiest villages in the Dartmoor National Park. It has some wonderful thatched cottages and a fine church. There are numerous footpaths in the parish and a popular walk is out to and through Lustleigh Cleave, a spectacular steep-sided valley near the village.

Buckland-in-the-Moor

Situated between Ashburton and Widecombe, this is yet another lovely place and a favourite with photographers, who do not seem able to resist this cluster of thatched cottages. The church clock at Buckland is unusual in the respect that instead of having numerals it has letters. Those with a keen eye will see that they spell out the message 'My Dear Mother'. Opposite are some cute ponies photographed on Roborough Down, an open common near Yelverton.

Lydford Gorge

Opposite are two pictures of Lydford Gorge (National Trust), one showing the famous White Lady Waterfall. This spectacular wooded valley is open to the public during the season and for anyone who enjoys an exciting walk, a visit is thoroughly recommended. On this page is the same river Lyd, high on the moor, a few miles above the ancient village of Lydford.

High Above the Lyd

There is some glorious walking country in the area shown in this picture, which was taken from Widgery Cross, on Brat Tor (shown opposite), looking towards Hare Tor, but as it's part of the Willsworthy Firing Range it is advisable to check firing times before planning any ramble. The cross was constructed at the expense of William Widgery, a talented Dartmoor artist, who wished to commemorate the Golden Jubilee of Queen Victoria in 1887. The picture on the right of the opposite page shows the River Avon just above Shipley Bridge, on the southern side of Dartmoor.

Vixen Tor
This tor near Merrivale is believed to be the highest, from summit to base, on the Moor. It was once the home of 'Vixana the Witch', who delighted in ensnaring wayfarers in the mire below it. A young and brave moorman was hired to remove her and in order to do so he was endowed with certain magical powers. More details of this and many other Dartmoor folk tales can be found in Dark and Dastardly Dartmoor.

Postbridge

This famous granite clapper bridge spans the East Dart river. Despite the strength of this stout and sturdy structure, it has been the victim of flood damage on a number of occasions, Dartmoor's rivers always rising rapidly after heavy downpours of rain. This cyclopean clapper bridge is a great attraction and one of the most photographed features in Devon.

Huccaby Bridge

This bridge spans the West Dart river only a short way upstream of Dartmeet. Before it reaches one of the Moor's most famous beauty spots, the river runs around a giant loop, almost doubling back on itself.

Dartmeet

This, as the place-name states, is the point where the two tributaries East and West Dart unite their flows to form the Double Dart. This picture of the boulder-strewn river was taken just below their confluence. As stepping stones these natural rocks in Darmoor's streams and rivers can often be slippery, so be careful!

The Dart and Buckfast Abbey

The Dart wends its way off open moorland, passing into a deep, green, wooded valley as seen here just above Holne Bridge. Opposite is a series of stepping stones, many miles upstream, at Sherberton on the West Dart river. Having been placed here at convenient intervals they provide a safe passage across, most of the time. Buckfast Abbey, on the edge of the Dartmoor National Park, is also shown opposite. Again a visit is thoroughly recommended.

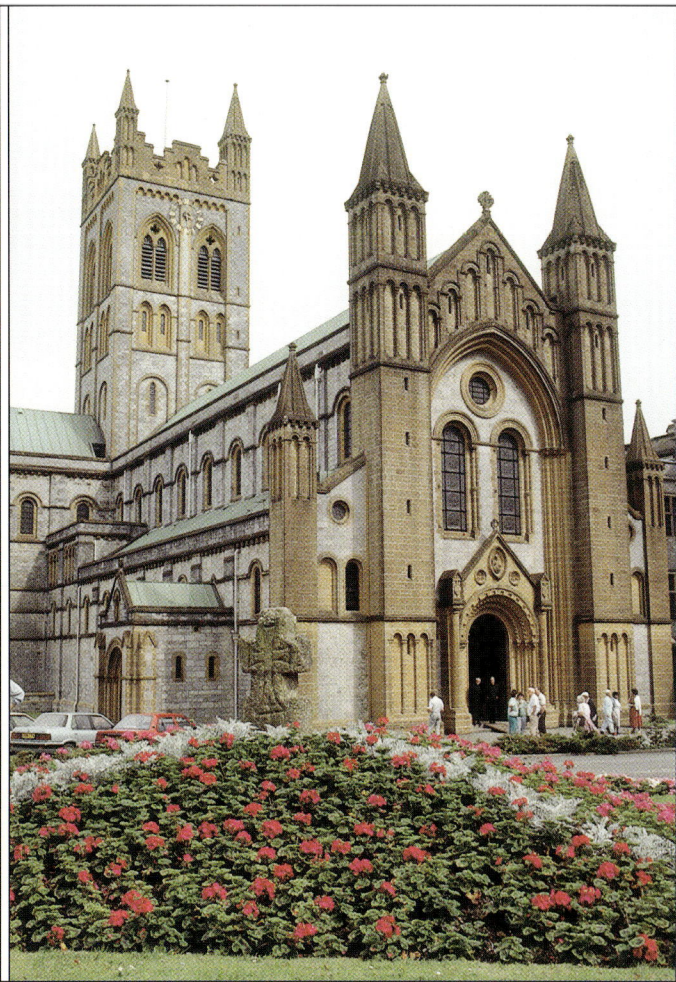

Horrabridge and Chagford

Above is the moorland-edge settlement of Horrabridge on the River Walkham, famed for its salmon and trout fishing and a tributary of the River Tavy, which it joins a few miles downstream at Double Waters. This village is surrounded by excellent walking country. Opposite are two pictures of the inland resort of Chagford, located on slopes above the River Teign, where fishing, walking and other outdoor pursuits are also popular. The strange structure shown in the left picture is the Market House, often referred to as 'The Pepperpot', a building that stands in The Square and which performs many functions. The Buller's Arms, named after a Boer War hero, is a floral reminder of how well this moorland settlement has done in 'Britain in Bloom' competitions. Chagford has two amazing, long-established ironmonger businesses. These, in their own way, are major attractions, people travelling many miles to shop in them.

Steps Bridge, Fingle Bridge and Castle Drogo

Above, it's Spring time at Steps Bridge, where the Teign approaches the edge of the Dartmoor National Park.

Opposite is the famed beauty spot of Fingle Bridge, some four miles upstream. A pleasant footpath follows the river, most of the way, between these two bridges, passing Clifford Bridge along the way. The picture beside it is taken from Sharp Tor, high on the northern side of the Teign Gorge a little less than a mile upstream from Fingle Bridge. It can be reached by walking the Hunters' Path. Castle Drogo (National Trust), near Drewsteignton, is just about visible on the top right side on the shoulder of the hill. Close-up it looks ancient, but it isn't and a visit will reveal all. Without doubt it should feature in any visitor's itinerary.

Moretonhampstead and Clearbrook

Above, the single terrace shown in the picture is, more or less, all that makes up the hamlet of Clearbrook on the edge of Roborough Down. Opposite is Moretonhampstead, a busy settlement, as seen from the heights of Mardon Down and also how it looks from the end of Court Street. The tall church tower of St Andrew's appears in both views.

The Land of Pixies!

Dartmoor is inhabited by a peculiar race of hyper-active tiny folk known as pixies. They have little dress sense, preferring their 'uniform' of red and green. Their favourite habitats include Sheeps Tor, shown in the right distance of the picture above, just beyond Burrator Reservoir. This was the first reservoir built on the moor and supplies the Plymouth area. The right-hand picture opposite was taken at Pixieland, where the pixies come in a vast variety of shapes and sizes. There are even ones here who have shunned their traditional 'clobber' to sport the colours of soccer players from the Premiership! On the left side, opposite, is the former post office at Peter Tavy, near Tavistock, with some of its customers patiently waiting for opening time!

Two Bridges

The two main roads which criss-cross high Dartmoor do so at Two Bridges. Here, at this important crossroads beside the West Dart river, is a hotel which has catered for wayfarers and visitors for many years. The Oscar-winning star of Gone With the Wind (1939), Vivien Leigh, who was famously married to Laurence Olivier (from 1940 to 1960), was earlier married to a Dawlish man, Leigh Holman. Her stage name is said to derive from his name. They met, it's believed, at a hunt ball at the Two Bridges Hotel near Princetown, where there is still a 'Vivien Leigh Suite' named in her honour. She stayed here many times with her friend Jack Merrivale.

Dartmoor Prison, Princetown

To many people the word 'Dartmoor' is synonymous with its prison. The original War Depot was built to house French prisoners-of-war. It opened in 1808 and by 1812 also had about a thousand American prisoners-of-war. When the war ended Princetown became a ghost town and remained so for several decades, until the prison opened up to accommodate British convicts. The tall mast rising vertically behind the prison is on North Hessary Tor.

Hound Tor

The idea behind this book has been to give an impression, or flavour, of what Dartmoor is all about, an almost impossible task given the size and variety of this amazing place of mists, mires and moods. However, I hope that you will derive pleasure from looking at these pictures taken in different seasons and over a number of years. The view above was taken at Hound Tor on Eastern Dartmoor, one of the largest outcrops in the Dartmoor National Park.